Melodies

Birds Coloring Book

Spring and Forest, Hummingbirds, Parrots, Sparrows With Flowers, For Adults & Teenagers

Rachel Mintz

Join Our Coloring Books VIP Group
Members Get Giveaways, Deep Discount Offers,
Win Prizes – Visit Site To Join (It's Free)

www.ColoringBookHome.com

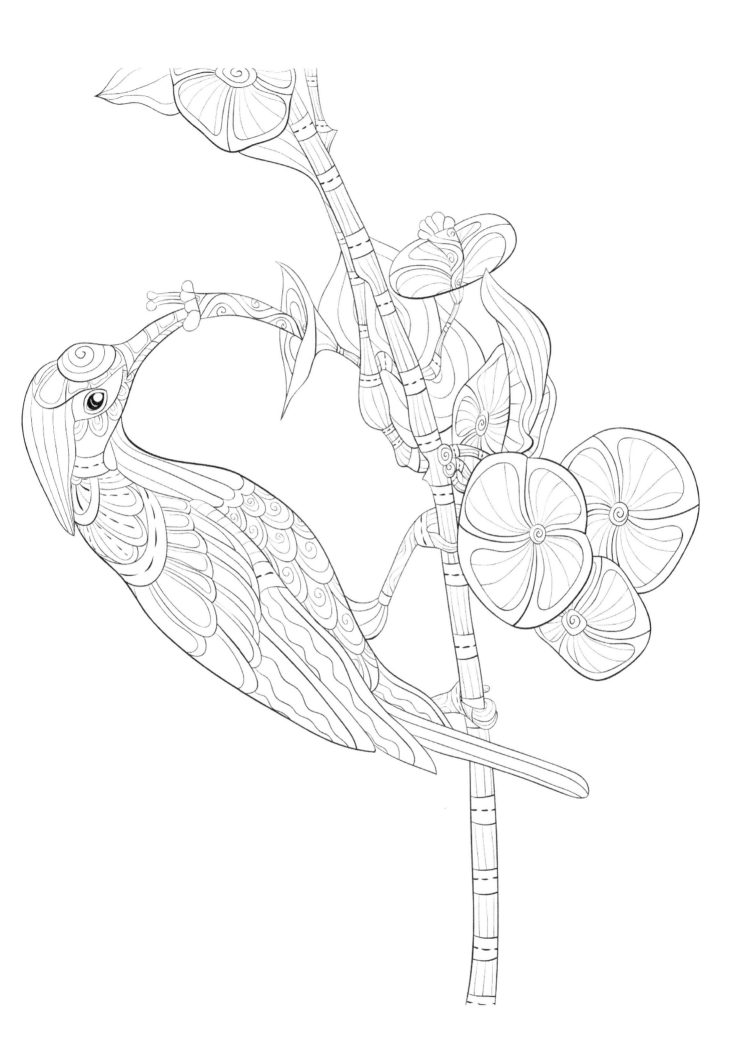

Thank you for coloring with us

Please rate & review

Cutie Friends
Doodle Pets Coloring Book

For Kids
Ages 6-10

Rachel Mintz

Nectar Birds

Hummingbirds
Coloring Book   Rachel Mintz

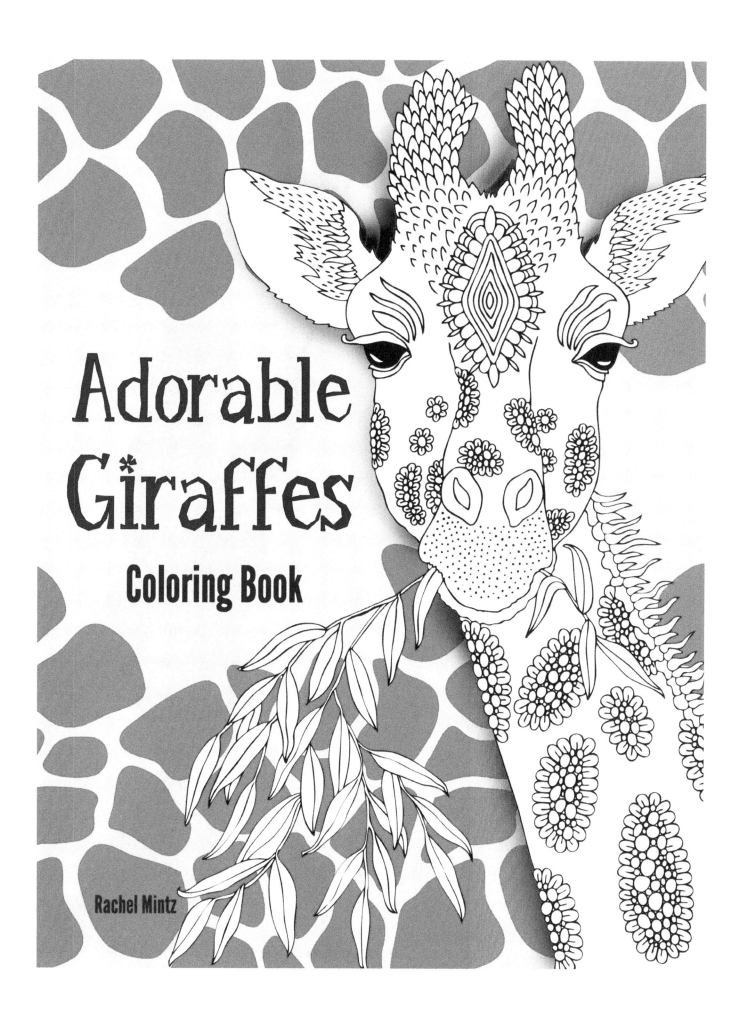

Adorable Giraffes

Coloring Book

Rachel Mintz

Join Our Coloring Books VIP Group
Members Get Giveaways, Deep Discount Offers,
Win Prizes – Visit Site To Join (It's Free)

www.ColoringBookHome.com

Thank you for coloring with us

Please rate & review

Made in the USA
Coppell, TX
24 August 2021

61136910R00044